GET INFORMED—STAY INFORMED

EDUCATION EQUALITY

Heather C. Hudak

CRABTREE
PUBLISHING COMPANY
WWW.CRABTREEBOOKS.COM

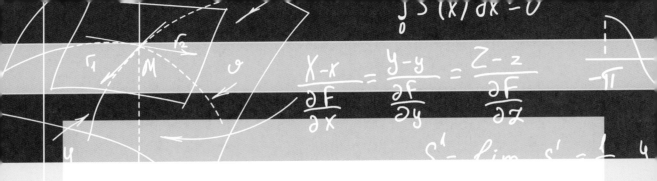

Author: Heather C. Hudak
Series research and development:
  Reagan Miller
Editor-in-chief: Lionel Bender
Editors: Simon Adams, Ellen Rodger
Proofreaders: Laura Booth,
  Crystal Sikkens
Project coordinator: Melissa Boyce
Design and photo research:
  Ben White
Production: Kim Richardson
**Production coordinator and
  Prepress technician:** Margaret Amy Salter
Print coordinator: Katherine Berti
Consultant: Emily Drew,
  Public Librarian, B.F.A., M.S.-LIS

Produced for Crabtree
Publishing Company by
Bender Richardson White

Photographs and reproductions:
Alamy 4–5 (Richard Levine), 11 (Entertainment Pictures), Stock
Photo, 12–13 (Bob Daemmrich), 16–17 (Art Directors & TRIP),
31 (RosaIreneBetancourt9), 32–33 (Jim Newberry); Bloomsbury
Publishing: 19 (Illustration by Ekua Holmes, courtesy of Bloomsbury
Publishing); Getty Images: 7 (NurPhoto), 8–9 (Mark Wilson), 12–13
(Ron Bull), 14–15 (Mohamed Abdiwahab), 34–35 (Portland Press
Herald), 36–37 (Drew Angerer), 38–39 (Giles Clarke), 42–43 (Steve
Russell); Library of Congress: 24 (Farm Security Administration/Office
of War Information Photograph Collection), Shutterstock: 1, 26–27
(Jacob Lund), 6–7 (Syda Productions), 10 (Fabio Principe), 28 (Monkey
Business Images), 29 (stock_photo_world), 32–33 (Sheila Fitzgerald),
35, 40–41 (Rawpixel.com); Topfoto 20, 21, 24–25 (Granger NYC), 23
(World History Archive); Icons & heading band: shutterstock.com

Diagrams: Stefan Chabluk, using the following as sources of data:
p. 6 U.S. News/National Center for Education Statistics. p. 17 Our
World in Data/United Nations. p. 18 Annual Survey of School System
Finances, Census Bureau. p. 23 Map based on U.S. National Archives
data. p. 25 Statista.com/U.S. Board of Education. p. 30 National Center
for Education Statistics. p. 35 www.usnews.com. p. 39 Census of
Population, Statistics Canada.

Library and Archives Canada Cataloguing in Publication

Title: Education equality / Heather C. Hudak.
Names: Hudak, Heather C., 1975- author.
Series: Get informed--stay informed.
Description: Series statement: Get informed, stay informed |
  Includes bibliographical references and index.
Identifiers: Canadiana (print) 20190240687 |
  Canadiana (ebook) 20190236744 |
  ISBN 9780778772729 (hardcover) |
  ISBN 9780778772767 (softcover) |
  ISBN 9781427124654 (HTML)
Subjects: LCSH: Educational equalization—Juvenile literature. |
  LCSH: Discrimination in education—
  Juvenile literature. | LCSH: Academic achievement—
  Juvenile literature.
Classification: LCC LC213 .H83 2020 | DDC j379.2/6—dc23

Library of Congress Cataloging-in-Publication Data

CIP available at the Library of Congress

LCCN: 2019053212

Crabtree Publishing Company

www.crabtreebooks.com   1-800-387-7650

Printed in the U.S.A./032020/CG20200127

Published in Canada
Crabtree Publishing
616 Welland Ave.
St. Catharines, ON
L2M 5V6

Published in the United States
Crabtree Publishing
PMB 59051
350 Fifth Avenue, 59th Floor
New York, NY 10118

Published in the United Kingdom
Crabtree Publishing
Maritime House
Basin Road North, Hove
BN41 1WR

Published in Australia
Crabtree Publishing
Unit 3 – 5 Currumbin Court
Capalaba
QLD 4157

CONTENTS

If there is one thing most countries accept and acknowledge, it is that education is a **fundamental** right. Access to education helps ensure that children can achieve their full **potential**. It helps them develop the knowledge and skills they need to secure jobs and make sound decisions about life events. In turn, well-educated youth grow up to become active contributors to **society**, which helps their communities grow and thrive.

> *Until we get equality in education, we won't have an equal society.*
> Sonia Sotomayor, U.S. Supreme Court justice, 2011

THE OL' COLLEGE LIE

Lori Loughlin of "Fuller House" allegedly paid to help daughters Olivia Jade (left) and Isabella Rose (right) get into USC by pretending to be good at rowing.

Wealthy charged with corrupt conspiracy to get kids into top universities

Thirty-three wealthy parents, including two Hollywood actresses, are accused of paying a man to cheat on standardized tests or fake an athletic career to get their kids into exclusive colleges.

PAGES 4-11

BUYER LEARNING

▲ Education equality hit the headlines in the United States in March 2019 when some wealthy people tried to buy their children an unfair advantage in the education system.

In recent times, there have been huge strides in improving education opportunities globally. In 1998, there were an estimated 381 million children out of school. By 2018, the number had dropped to about 258 million, or one in seven of the world's 1.98 billion children. However, there is still a long way to go before all children around the world have **equal** opportunities for education.

In countries such as Yemen and Nigeria, internal conflict has destroyed schools or made them unsafe for children to attend. In Iran, women cannot take certain courses in college such as engineering, as the government feels they should focus more on their families. In Mali, Chad, and Ethiopia only boys go to school, not girls. The girls must go to work or stay at home and help care for their families.

STAYING SAFE

According to the **United Nations** (UN) Universal Declaration of Human Rights, people of each and every age, race, gender, ability, social class, and religion should be treated as equals when it comes to education. Most developed nations offer free public schools to do this. However, not everyone is equal. In order for students to truly achieve their full potential and receive a quality education, they need to be treated **equitably**.

When there is equity in education, students are assessed to find out if they have any unique needs that, if nothing is done, will keep them from doing well in school. Equity in education calls for support systems to be put in place that ensure every child has an equal chance of success in life.

In North America, all children have the right to equal educational opportunities whatever their background, their parents' wealth, where they live, or if they are citizens or new **immigrants**. Yet students in the United States, Canada, and Mexico still experience large achievement gaps from one school or community to another. Factors within and beyond the schools create inequality when it comes to student success.

WEALTH, CULTURE, AND INEQUALITY

Inequality happens at all levels of education, from kindergarten to college and university. In the spring of 2019, dozens of people in the United States were arrested on suspicion of trying to bribe universities to accept their children despite their low academic grades. The admissions **controversy** caused many people to question if their children were being treated fairly in all levels of the school system.

In Canada in September 2019, the names of 2,800 **indigenous** children who died in **residential schools** across the country were put on display at the Canadian Museum of

▲ Equality of education tries to ensure that everyone, including people of each and every **marginalized** group, gets a good education.

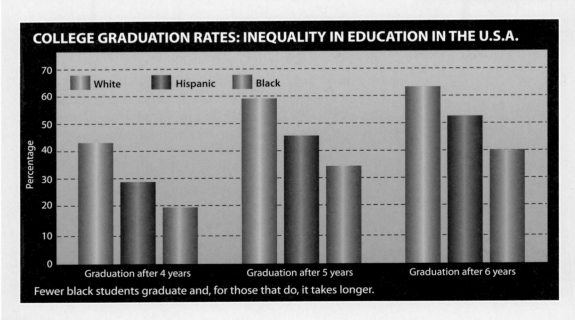

COLLEGE GRADUATION RATES: INEQUALITY IN EDUCATION IN THE U.S.A.

Legend: White, Hispanic, Black

Percentage (y-axis: 0 to 70)

Graduation after 4 years: White ~43, Hispanic ~29, Black ~20
Graduation after 5 years: White ~59, Hispanic ~46, Black ~35
Graduation after 6 years: White ~64, Hispanic ~53, Black ~41

Fewer black students graduate and, for those that do, it takes longer.

THE CENTRAL ISSUES

In most developed countries, free public education is paid for by the government. Why is it important for society to provide equal education opportunities for all children? How would it affect you and your family if there were no free public schools in your community?

> *More money is put into prisons than into schools. That, in itself, is the description of a nation bent on suicide. I mean, what is more precious to us than our own children? We are going to build a lot more prisons if we do not deal with the schools and their inequalities.*
> Jonathan Kozol, American writer, educator, and activist, 2005

History in Gatineau, Quebec. From the late 1800s to the mid-1990s, more than 150,000 indigenous children were forcibly removed from their families and placed in government-funded residential schools. They were forced to give up their culture and beliefs and **assimilate** to European ways of life. The schools were not equal to others across Canada. They lacked proper facilities and supplies, and teachers were poorly qualified. Students were poorly treated and experienced **discrimination.**

WHY THE TOPIC IS IMPORTANT

Getting informed and staying informed about **current affairs**, such as education equality, will help you understand how they impact on your own life. Having a well-balanced viewpoint will also help you make informed decisions about how best to support education equality for everyone in North America and across the globe.

▼ In April 2019, students, teachers, and parents protested in support of Philadelphia's City Council tax that helped pay for poor and middle-class children to go to early education programs.

HOW TO GET INFORMED

To understand an issue, such as education equality, you need to know the **context**. Context refers to the background or history of a topic. It provides details about the setting, environment, or framework for an event, statement, or idea. It helps you understand how the issue has changed over time. It also tells you how past events have shaped the issue in the present day. When you know the context, you can make sense of information, words, and concepts you may not otherwise understand. Context also tells us how factors, such as the culture and ideas of the time, may impact people's views about the issue.

▶ Most U.S. states do not have a law to protect against **LGBTQ** discrimination. In a March 2019 press conference, Nancy Pelosi, Speaker of the U.S. House of Representatives, unveiled the Equality Act of 2019 bill, which included the banning of discrimination—including in education—on the basis of gender identity and sexual orientation.

Equity refers to acting in a fair and reasonable way so that everyone receives equal treatment.

Equality happens when all members of society have the same rights, status, and opportunities.

Marginalized is the term used to describe a group of racially, culturally, or ethnically distinct people who are treated by the majority as unimportant and are often excluded in society.

Discrimination is the unfair treatment of a person due to their race, religion, age, gender, ability, or other factors.

Prejudice is an unfair feeling of dislike or a poor opinion of a person because of their race, religion, age, gender, ability, or other factors.

Underserved means there are not enough services or facilities to provide proper support.

Achievement gaps happen when there are ongoing differences between the performance scores of different groups of people, such as students who come from high-income or low-income households.

BACKGROUND KNOWLEDGE

To build context, you need background knowledge of the issue. This is the basic information you require to understand how to research the issue and build up a complete picture of it. It involves learning about where, when, and how the issue started, and who the key players are. In order to understand why education equality is a top priority for most countries, it is important to learn about events and changes in society that led to the current views and **perspectives** on the issue.

You can get background knowledge by studying such documents and reports as:

- a high-level **summary** of the topic
- definitions of important words and concepts
- a general overview of key issues
- government statements and initiatives
- a list of experts who can provide deeper insight into the topic
- important dates related to the issue.

SOURCE MATERIALS

Source materials can help you build your background knowledge and answer any questions you might have about education equality. There are two key types of source materials: primary sources and secondary sources. Primary sources are first-hand accounts of an event. They are original materials, created at the time of the event or by people who had a direct connection to it. Secondary sources are reports and summaries mostly based on primary evidence. For your studies, use a mix of both sources.

Sometimes, primary sources include **bias**, or the creator's personal thoughts or feelings about the issue. Other sources, like those based on scientific research, present straight facts and figures. Primary sources created closer to the event tend to be more accurate, as people may not recall the details as clearly or have the same point of view as time passes.

Primary sources on the issue include:

- social media posts by political leaders about the status of school programs
- eyewitness accounts from teachers who have worked at both underserved and well-funded schools

- **statistics** and data on achievement scores
- school or college **prospectuses** used to promote the school to potential students and parents
- a report created by a career counselor about graduation rates and college applicants
- laws about education equality.

Secondary sources are created by people who do not have direct experience with an event or issue. They are made by analyzing, describing, or summarizing other source materials, including primary sources. Textbooks, biographies, newspaper and magazine articles written after an event, and reference books are all examples of secondary source materials. When researching education equality, these sources may include brochures written by educational charities that provide support to **underprivileged** youth or a **curriculum** outlining the courses offered at a school.

SELECTING MATERIALS

A good and convenient place to look for information about education equality is the Internet. Here you can find books, blogs, documents, videos, photos, interviews, and panel discussions. However, the quality of the content varies. Anyone can post online whether or not they are experts on a topic. As a result, the information may be

▲ Newspapers—printed and online—are a good source of the lastest news, reports, announcements, and investigations on a topic or issue such as education equality.

out of date, filled with errors, or contain personal opinions rather than facts. Be mindful of these issues when using search engines and Internet databases to locate source materials.

Libraries and local archives are other great places to look for source materials that you cannot find anywhere else such as old school newspapers and yearbooks. Librarians can help you locate and record high-quality information from a variety of sources.

RESEARCH TIPS

Researching a topic can be intimidating. These tips can help make it easier to learn about education equality:

- Find experts on the topic and see what they are saying about it.
- Do a targeted Internet search using keywords, events, and concepts.
- Make sure any journals or websites you use are created by trusted sources such as governments or education institutes.
- Look for visuals, such as graphs and charts, that help break down complex statistics and figures.
- Compare information from a variety of sources to ensure accuracy and verify facts and opinions.

▼ Below shows a scene from a 2010 documentary, *Waiting for "Superman,"* which highlighted many of the inequalities in the U.S. education system of the time. Using many perspectives, it illustrated how poverty affects education.

There is more information at our fingertips than ever before, so it is not enough to gather just any source materials. You must assess the quality of your sources to ensure they are valid, authentic, and trustworthy. When **evaluating** sources to determine if they are credible and worthwhile, ask yourself these questions:

- Does the creator have solid credentials? Is this person an expert on the topic or do they have education or experience related to it?
- Does it contain bias? Does it present a balanced point of view? Does it contain facts or opinions?
- When was it created? Is there a date on the source? Does it contain current information or is it clearly out of date? Is newer information available that is more relevant to the topic?
- If it includes quotations, statements, or statistics, can you verify these from other sources?
- Is the information geared toward a certain group of people who may share the same thoughts or feelings? Does the audience relate to the information in some way?
- Who published it? Does the publisher have anything to gain by putting out this information? Was it paid for by a special interest group or business?

If the source is old, contains errors and personal opinions, or tries to persuade you to feel a certain way, it may not be credible. Try to use up-to-date, unbiased sources that are based on facts.

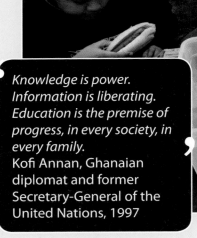

" Knowledge is power. Information is liberating. Education is the premise of progress, in every society, in every family. "
Kofi Annan, Ghanaian diplomat and former Secretary-General of the United Nations, 1997

▼ Charter schools, such as Peak Preparatory Academy in Dallas, Texas, create their own programming, decide which students to educate, and choose their own measures for assessing both teacher and student performance. (See pages 22–23 for more details on charter schools.)

GAINING PERSPECTIVE

It is important to use a variety of sources to ensure you have a balanced view of a topic. People interpret information in different ways

▲ In the United States, about 30 million students depend on federal government-subsidized free and low-cost lunches under the Healthy, Hunger-Free Kids Act of 2010. This is an example of a program that reinforces or aids educational equality based on the idea that if your belly is full, you can concentrate on learning.

and have different opinions and perspectives about issues. When it comes to education equality, some people believe all children should be treated the same regardless of their individual needs. They think all schools should have access to the exact same funding and resources even if some students require additional support to help them achieve success.

Others believe education equity is a better model. They think children who have special learning needs or those who come from underprivileged communities should have access to additional resources to help them succeed academically. Before you can make an informed decision about education equality, you need to consider many different viewpoints.

ASK YOUR OWN QUESTIONS

Some people include bias in their work without meaning to. Others intend to include it. Do you think it is possible to remove bias completely? What types of bias do you think are involved in education equality?

3 THE BIG PICTURE

The idea that everyone should have fair and equal access to a good-quality education is not a new one. In order to understand the big picture when it comes to education equality, it is important to know the history of equal education for all.

$$\frac{3}{4}$$

$$\sin \overline{\pi} \quad \lambda \overline{\pi} \quad 3\overline{\pi} \quad X$$

$$\frac{2}{4}$$

$$\frac{\sin 2x}{1 \cdot 3} + \frac{4\sin 4x}{3 \cdot 5} + \frac{6\sin 6x}{5 \cdot 7} + \dots \Big) \qquad \frac{1}{4}$$

Following World War II (1939–1945), leaders from around the world vowed to never let the **atrocities** that took place during that war happen again. Members of the United Nations began to draft a bill of human rights that outlined the basic rights and freedoms entitled to all people, no matter their status in society. On December 10, 1948, the UN General Assembly adopted the Universal Declaration of Human Rights (UDHR). Article 26 focuses specifically on the right to education. It says that "everyone has the right to education." It also states that "education shall be free, at least in the elementary or fundamental stages," and that "education shall be directed to the full development of the human personality . . . ."

SETTING STANDARDS

The UDHR is not a **binding law**. However, since it was put into action, countries and territories all over the world have shown their agreement and support by bringing in their own laws and policies on education equality. The governments of most nations include a framework for education within their **constitution**. Many of them promise to provide free education to every child. Others even make certain levels of education mandatory.

Some countries do not specifically outline education within their constitutions. One of these countries is the United States. Education is not mentioned within the U.S. constitution. In fact, the United States is one of the only **independent** countries in the world that does not fully support the UDHR. Canada does support it.

◄ Internally displaced and refugee youth often do not have access to education. At Badbaado refugee camp in Mogadishu, Somalia, children receive some free schooling from volunteer university students from several countries.

One of the main reasons education is not outlined in the U.S. constitution is because each state is responsible for deciding how best to approach education within its own borders. While free public education for all children is a **mandate** shared by the whole country, how each state chooses to carry out that requirement is different.

U.S. states vary on how they manage teachers, schools, funding, the curriculum, and so on. As a result, the quality of education is quite different in each state. However, the federal Department of Education aims to minimize inequality by overseeing education in each state. It sets out requirements for standard tests, minimum number of classroom hours, and required subjects of study, among other related things.

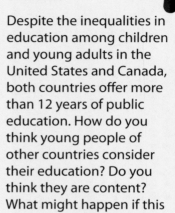

WHAT'S AT STAKE?

Despite the inequalities in education among children and young adults in the United States and Canada, both countries offer more than 12 years of public education. How do you think young people of other countries consider their education? Do you think they are content? What might happen if this inequality continues?

▶ Some students require additional support in school. For instance, a student who recently arrived from another country may require language assistance, or a student with a learning disability may need the help of a specially trained teacher to master certain skills.

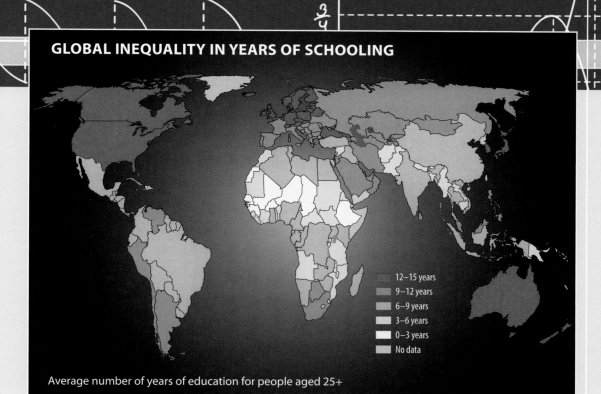

GLOBAL INEQUALITY IN YEARS OF SCHOOLING

12–15 years
9–12 years
6–9 years
3–6 years
0–3 years
No data

Average number of years of education for people aged 25+

CANADIAN EDUCATION RIGHTS

Canada outlines a framework for education within its constitution and its Charter of Rights and Freedoms. However, it does not have a federal department specifically to oversee education standards across the country. Instead, provincial and territorial governments have sole powers over funding, laws, and policies related to education. While education is a high priority across the country, funding models and the quality of education vary from one province to the next.

The federal government is responsible only for the education of indigenous peoples in Canada. Studies show that the federally funded schools receive less money per student than students in provincially funded school districts. Many indigenous communities lack resources, services, and facilities, and only 40 percent of indigenous youth graduate high school compared to 90 percent of nonindigenous youth.

From the earliest moments in recent North American history, education was withheld from **enslaved** people, women, and the poor. These people were seen as inferior. In this way, race and wealth have, and still do, play a significant role in education equality in the United States and Canada.

In the 1700s, enslaved people were not allowed to attend public schools in the Southern states, as it was believed they would pose a threat to their owners if they could read and write. In some states, it was even considered a crime to teach an enslaved person. However, some plantation owners had informal schools to educate the enslaved, who could help with record-keeping and other tasks. In the Northern states, education of the enslaved was allowed, and they were much more likely to be taught basic reading and writing skills.

INITIATIVES IN CANADA

Some U.S. enslaved people fled to Canada, where they were free to live as they chose. In 1849, a former owner, white minister William King, moved from Louisiana to the Elgin Settlement in western Canada. The next year, he founded the Buxton Mission School as a place for escaped enslaved people and free blacks to live and get an education.

The Elgin education model was unique. Most black settlers were taxed but not given equal opportunities. Africville was an African-Canadian community built outside of Halifax,

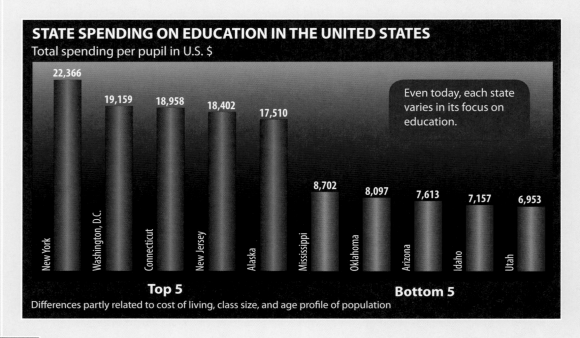

STATE SPENDING ON EDUCATION IN THE UNITED STATES
Total spending per pupil in U.S. $

22,366 — New York
19,159 — Washington, D.C.
18,958 — Connecticut
18,402 — New Jersey
17,510 — Alaska
8,702 — Mississippi
8,097 — Oklahoma
7,613 — Arizona
7,157 — Idaho
6,953 — Utah

Even today, each state varies in its focus on education.

Top 5   **Bottom 5**

Differences partly related to cost of living, class size, and age profile of population

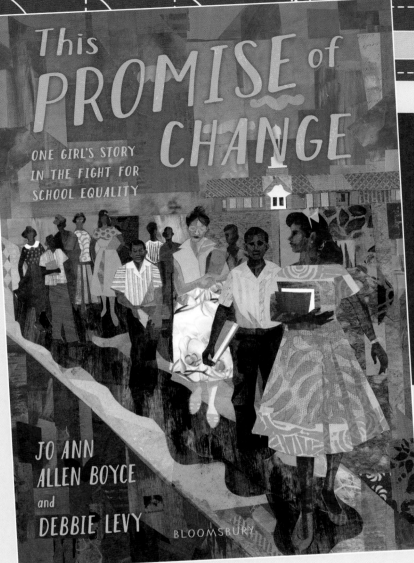

This Promise of Change: One Girl's Story in the Fight for School Equality

JO ANN ALLEN BOYCE and DEBBIE LEVY

BLOOMSBURY

◄ *This Promise of Change* is the story of 14-year-old Jo Ann Allen Boyce, one of 12 African-American students who integrated in a white high school in Tennessee in 1956. It is based on original research and interviews with people involved in fighting the color barrier of the time in education.

Nova Scotia, in the mid-1700s. The local community school closed in 1953 and students were bused into Halifax to attend mostly white schools. Africvillians faced discrimination at the schools and were not given the same access to resources as white students.

OPPORTUNITY AWAITS

The U.S. **Emancipation Proclamation** was signed into effect by President Abraham Lincoln in 1863. Two years later, the Bureau of Refugees, Freedmen, and Abandoned Lands was created to provide food, housing, and education to poor people of all races living in the South amid the aftermath of the American Civil War (1861–1865). Thousands of black schools were established to help newly freed enslaved people build the skills they needed to transition into regular society.

CONSTITUTIONAL CHANGE

The 14th Amendment to the U.S. Constitution came into effect in 1868. It maintains that all children have the right to equal educational opportunity and cannot be denied that right for any reason. Civil rights laws were put into place to enforce it. However, many of the states that once allowed people to be enslaved looked for ways to get around these laws. They said that equality could be achieved even if races were kept separate.

These states used "separate but equal" and **segregation** as a policy or **doctrine** for everything from schools to voting rights, buses, restaurants, and drinking fountains. Despite the fact that African-Americans were to be treated as equals under the constitution, the services they received, such as school funding, were typically of much lower quality than those provided to white Americans.

ASK YOUR OWN QUESTIONS

What is meant by the term "separate but equal"? Who did it apply to? Why did the Supreme Court deem it unconstitutional? How did it inspire civil rights laws?

▼ The first black students to be admitted to Little Rock Central High School in Little Rock, Arkansas, in 1957 were known as the Little Rock Nine. They were given a military escort due to the prejudice and discrimination they faced from hostile white locals.

> In these days, it is doubtful that any child may reasonably be expected to succeed in life if [he] is denied the opportunity of an education.
>
> Chief Justice Earl Warren on the *Brown v. Board of Education* ruling, 1954

▲ On May 18, 1954, the cover of *The New York Times* announced the Supreme Court decision in the *Brown v. Board of Education* school segregation case.

BROWN VERSUS BOARD OF EDUCATION

Until the mid-1900s, racial segregation was common in schools across the United States. In 1951, the parents of 20 black children in Topeka, Kansas, filed a lawsuit against the local board of education. They said black schools were separate but not equal, and they promoted the unfair treatment of black Americans. One parent, Olivia L. Brown, explained that her daughter had to travel far by bus to a segregated school even though there was a white school just seven blocks away.

Although the district court ruled against the parents, the U.S. Supreme Court overturned the ruling in 1954. Chief Justice Earl Warren stated that even if black schools were equal, the concept of separating blacks from whites in itself was unconstitutional and a violation of the 14th Amendment. It would transform education equality.

KEY INFORMATION

Segregation refers to the act of setting people of different races apart from one another. **Desegregation** was the end of racial segregation. **Integration** brought people of all races together as a whole.

It took decades to get rid of segregation in U.S. schools. But even today, race and social status play a major role in education equality across the country. One of the reasons for this is because the U.S. federal government only contributes to eight to nine percent of school budgets. Public education is largely funded through local property taxes that are used only within the communities where they are collected.

People who live in high-income communities pay higher taxes, which leads to better-funded schools and a higher quality of education for children living there. People living in lower-income communities—which tend to have a higher presence of African-American and marginalized youth—pay lower taxes, resulting in underfunded schools and a lower quality of education. As a result, black and marginalized children are less likely to climb above their current social status (see page 30).

CASE STUDY

In Boston, desegregation and integration were done through a complex busing system from 1974 to 1988. Thousands of black and white students were sent to schools in neighborhoods far from their homes as a way to ensure a balance of races at each school. The system received backlash from white parents, and many Boston schools are still not racially balanced today.

SOLUTIONS TO THE PROBLEM

The following types of schools have been set up to solve such problems, but each has pros and cons. They are funded in different ways (see panel opposite).

- Private schools charge tuition for students to attend, which typically means that only people who can afford to pay get to attend these schools. Class sizes tend to be small, giving teachers more opportunity to focus on individual student needs. They have higher standards for teacher qualifications and better access to resources such as textbooks.
- Charter schools were originally created to help low-performing students with poor reading skills have a better chance at success in school. They look for **alternative** styles of instruction that might help children overcome obstacles they face in traditional learning environments. However, few charter schools are located in lower-income urban centers where the need is greatest. The time or cost of traveling to the school makes it challenging for underprivileged children to attend.
- Magnet schools cater mainly to students who excel in their studies. They often focus on providing the arts, technology, or other dedicated fields of study to students who are gifted in that field. They give those individuals a better chance to further hone their skills in a way that not all students receive.

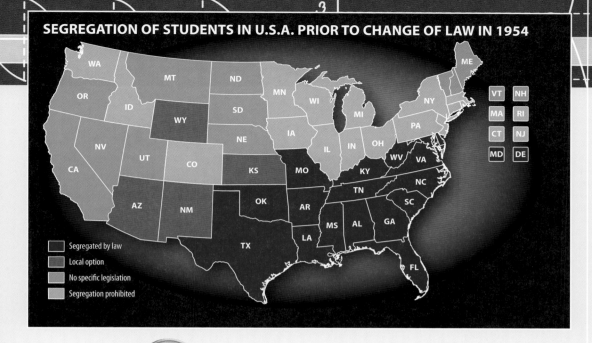

SEGREGATION OF STUDENTS IN U.S.A. PRIOR TO CHANGE OF LAW IN 1954

- Segregated by law
- Local option
- No specific legislation
- Segregation prohibited

FUNDING

Public schools are free for all children to attend. They are paid for using government or public funds.

Private schools do not receive money from the government. They are paid for by private organizations or through fees charged to attend them.

Charter schools receive public funding, but they do not fall under the same laws and regulations as public schools. Each school is privately managed and provides unique course offerings based on its own mandate, or charter.

Magnet schools are similar to charter schools. However, they are managed by the state public school system and must meet state standards.

▲ This image shows a racially segregated classroom at a white school in 1967. Most schools were not fully integrated until many years after the *Brown v. Board of Education* decision.

Across North America, women were treated as less than equal for many centuries. They were not allowed to vote, own property, or earn a fair wage. Most people thought there was not much purpose for educating women as they rarely worked outside the house. During the 1800s, women began to push for better education rights, and **post-secondary** institutions started to open their doors to them.

Even into the late 1900s, high schools often segregated boys and girls within schools or offered different curricula based on gender. Boys were encouraged to study subjects such as math and science so they could become doctors, lawyers, or engineers. Many schools placed girls in **home economics** programs that taught them to be good homemakers rather than to prepare them for post-secondary studies.

LEVELING THE FIELD

In 1972, President Richard Nixon signed Title IX into effect to help stop gender discrimination in federally funded education programs. As a result, any school that received money from the federal government had to start treating both genders equally in all subject areas, including athletics. Traditionally, male athletics programs had much bigger budgets for better facilities and equipment. Now, female athletics programs were given access to the same funds. Since 1972, the number of female high-school athletes has increased from about 300,000 to more than 2.6 million.

Two years after Title IX was put in place, Nixon brought in the Equal Educational Opportunities Act (EEOA) of 1974. The act banned discrimination based on race, nationality, color, or sex against faculty, staff, and students. It called on educators to ensure equal opportunities for all people and for school districts to take steps to overcome obstacles to students' equal participation in school.

▼ In the 1940s, boys were urged to take math and science courses that would prepare them for post-secondary schooling and professional careers.

THE CENTRAL ISSUES

Segregation by race and gender were common until the late 1900s. How did this impact equal education rights? How has it shaped society today? Can you think of any similar forms of discrimination that take place in schools now?

While the EEOA was a step forward, gender-based discrimination persists today and extends to a broader discussion of LGBTQ rights in education. A survey conducted by the National Public Radio (NPR) showed that the education of LGBTQ students is negatively impacted by the **harassment**, bullying, and discrimination they face at school. In fact, 43 percent of LGBTQ people who responded to the survey said that LGBTQ students do not have the same opportunity for a quality education as other students.

▼ Female students are seen here in a cooking class at Bethesda–Chevy Chase High School in Maryland, in 1935. Then, girls were often taught skills that would help them manage a family.

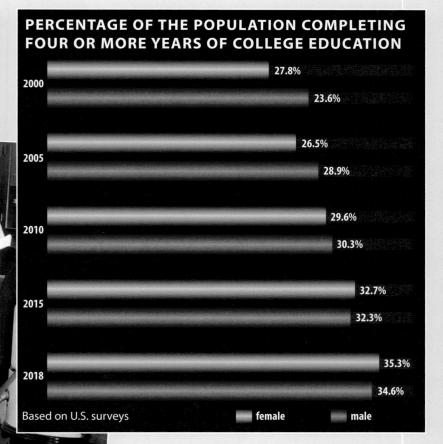

PERCENTAGE OF THE POPULATION COMPLETING FOUR OR MORE YEARS OF COLLEGE EDUCATION

Year	female	male
2000	27.8%	23.6%
2005	26.5%	28.9%
2010	29.6%	30.3%
2015	32.7%	32.3%
2018	35.3%	34.6%

Based on U.S. surveys

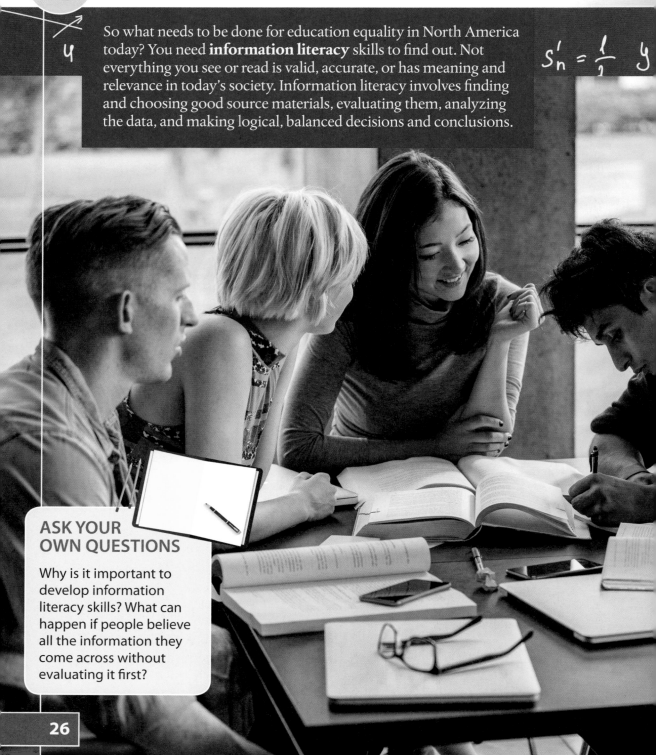

4 AN INFORMED DECISION

So what needs to be done for education equality in North America today? You need **information literacy** skills to find out. Not everything you see or read is valid, accurate, or has meaning and relevance in today's society. Information literacy involves finding and choosing good source materials, evaluating them, analyzing the data, and making logical, balanced decisions and conclusions.

$$s'_n = \frac{1}{n} \quad y$$

y

ASK YOUR OWN QUESTIONS

Why is it important to develop information literacy skills? What can happen if people believe all the information they come across without evaluating it first?

▼ It is good to talk with other people about their views and experience of education equality. It can help broaden your perspective. Your view may support or oppose the common opinion but, if you are well informed, your view matters just as much.

DEVELOP YOUR SKILLS

Imagine you want to know more about education equality for physically disabled students in North America and how their needs are being met. Where would you begin?

Use these tips to find, sort, and evaluate information critically and competently:

• Before you start looking for information, clearly define your scope and objective. Otherwise, you will waste time sorting through unnecessary details. Physical disabilities is a broad subject. Brainstorm ideas and then come up with a list of questions you want to answer.

• Start searching for sources. Type keywords, such as "wheelchair ramp funding," into a search engine on the Internet. Look through newspapers and magazines or visit the local library for data. Talk to experts on the topic, watch documentary films, and search databases for information. When you find a source that helps answer your questions, record its details. That way you can easily locate it again later if you need more information.

• Assess the sources you find to see if they are valid. Can you find the same information in more than one source? If so, it is likely true. A public announcement on a school website, a write-up in a student association report, or an interview with a local congressperson are examples of credible sources for your topic.

• Share the information. Write an essay, produce a podcast, or give a presentation to tell others about what you have learned. Refine your report based on their feedback.

THE VALUE OF EDUCATION

There are many different points of view on education equality, both positive and negative. Using your information literacy skills, consider as many of these as you can. Ensure you have the facts and not only opinions. Thoroughly understand all aspects of the issue before drawing conclusions about it.

IMPACT OF POOR EDUCATION

Despite efforts to educate youth in all parts of the world, many students lack access to quality education. As such, they are not gaining the skills they need to lead successful and fulfilling lives.

For instance, approximately 750 million adults around the world do not have basic reading and writing skills. About two thirds of these are women. Without the ability to read, it is not possible to master simple tasks such as filling out a job application, casting a vote in an election, or finding directions on a map.

▼ In most developed nations, governments provide some form of free public education and require children to attend school for a certain number of years. When people are more knowledgeable and skilled, they are more active citizens and contribute to the greater good.

> "Education is the passport to the future, for tomorrow belongs to those who prepare for it today."
> Malcolm X, human rights activist, 1964

▲ For governments, funding for education, including universities, has to compete with health, welfare, and other social services. Education equality is not always top priority.

BENEFITS FROM EDUCATION

Education has a value for society as a whole. Studies reveal that people who have access to quality primary and secondary education are more likely to find gainful employment, have a stable family life, and have better decision-making skills. They are more likely to be active citizens and take part in the voting process. When employment rates increase, so does tax revenue. These are all good things.

STARTLING FACTS

In places where quality education is lacking, there are more serious crimes, higher demands on public health-care systems, and increased enrollment in **welfare** assistance programs. In the United States, more than 40 percent of people in the prison system have not graduated from high school. Each one costs the government more than $30,000 dollars a year in expenses, while the average annual cost of public education is only $11,000 per child.

Globally, poverty levels could be decreased by more than 50 percent with improved access to secondary education for all. In addition, individual income earnings increase by 10 percent for each extra year of schooling. Overall, investing in public education is much more cost-effective than paying for the social and economic issues that come along with underfunded and low-quality school systems.

AN INSIGHT INTO INEQUALITIES

Inequity between wealthier and poorer communities plays a significant role in education equality. In many parts of Canada and the United States, high-quality education is limited to people who can afford it, either because they live in a middle- or upper-middle-class community with better funding for education, or because they pay for private schooling.

EVIDENCE FROM FACTS AND FIGURES

Statistics show that 45 percent of high-poverty schools in the United States receive less funding than other schools in the area. These schools spend about 16 percent less per student than even low-income schools. This has a huge impact on the overall quality of education.

THE CENTRAL ISSUES

Some students depend on support such as extra help from educators and meal assistance to help them succeed. While this is not equal, it is equitable. Should programs and assistance be provided to students who require additional support in school? Should taxpayers—including those who don't have children—pay for some children to be given special treatment? Why, or why not?

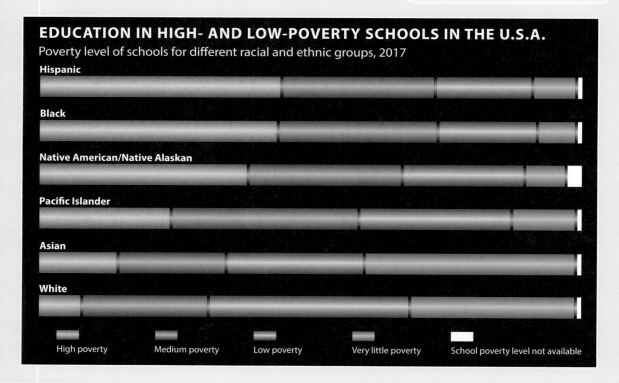

EDUCATION IN HIGH- AND LOW-POVERTY SCHOOLS IN THE U.S.A.
Poverty level of schools for different racial and ethnic groups, 2017

Hispanic

Black

Native American/Native Alaskan

Pacific Islander

Asian

White

High poverty | Medium poverty | Low poverty | Very little poverty | School poverty level not available

▲ On average, students enrolled in private schools tend to achieve higher scores on standardized tests than children who go to public schools.

" *An investment in knowledge pays the best interest.* Benjamin Franklin, U.S. Founding Father, 1758 "

Many underserved schools have a higher marginalized population. This results in a type of segregation that often means poor and marginalized students find themselves in disadvantaged schools with lower educational performance ratings. It makes it harder for them to overcome education inequalities. Only about 22 percent of black Americans go on to earn college degrees compared to 41 percent of white Americans. Black graduates are twice as likely to remain jobless after graduation.

POOR ACHIEVEMENT SCORES

Connecticut is one of the wealthiest U.S. states and is home to some of the best—and worst—schools in the country. In Greenwich, a high-income community, schools receive about $6,000 more per student than those in the low-income community of Bridgeport. Yet students in the Bridgeport area often need more help with their studies to overcome learning obstacles. As a result, achievement scores showed students in poorer Connecticut communities scored about 30 percent lower overall.

TEACHERS AND DROPOUTS

Teachers at underprivileged schools tend to be less experienced and lower paid. Some even lack appropriate teaching certifications. As a result, courses and curricula are often limited and less challenging than at schools with more funds.

Underserved schools have higher student dropout rates and fewer college graduates. Unemployment rates are more than double for high-school dropouts, and dropouts are more than three times as likely to receive support from government assistance programs that cost the government billions of dollars each year.

▶ In January 2019, more than 30,000 Los Angeles Unified School District (LAUSD) teachers went on strike. They wanted to draw attention to their cause, which included increasing funding to reduce class sizes; providing more counselors, nurses, and librarians in schools; and giving a raise in pay to educators. The LAUSD is the second-largest school district in the United States, and about 480,000 students were impacted by the strike.

▶ In February 2019, teachers in Oakland, California, went on strike in support of smaller class sizes and higher salaries.

How good—or bad—teachers are in helping children learn plays a big role in education equality. Students who have unskilled teachers may master less than 50 percent of the lessons taught in school. Meanwhile, students with good teachers can excel by a full grade level. Students with great teachers can gain 1.5 grade levels or more. A series of really great or bad teachers over time can lead to major differences in education quality and student achievement.

GOOD PAY AND OTHER WORK BENEFITS

The most experienced and qualified teachers are found in schools that offer the best teacher **compensation** packages. Salary, or pay, is a key part of the package. Teachers who are paid less may need to take a second job to add to their income. As a result, they have less time to spend preparing lessons, giving students support after school hours, and grading student work. Teachers also want good healthcare and pension benefits. The better the compensation package, the more likely a teacher might be to accept a role at a certain school. School districts in Canada and the United States that offer better packages are most often located in wealthier communities. This adds to the education problems faced by schools in poor and marginalized communities.

HIGH REGARD

Education equality also depends on a country's regard for teachers. In Singapore and Finland, for instance, the standards for teacher selection are very high. Only the best and the brightest students are accepted into teaching programs at colleges and universities. Upon graduation, only the top performers in those programs are offered teaching jobs. By contrast, in the United States, students need only slightly above-average grades to get into many teaching programs.

Students from both Singapore and Finland are known for their excellent results on international achievement exams. Yet, Finnish students spend only 600 hours per year in school compared to nearly 1,100 in most other countries. Their teachers spend the extra hours planning lessons well so that classroom time is highly effective. Singapore and Finland spend more of their national budget on education than do either the United States or Canada.

A country's teaching system can influence education equality as much as the schools and teachers. Nearly 40 percent of the gap in student achievement is due to tracking. This involves putting children in separate classes based on how they perform. Students who do really well in school are grouped in one class, while students who work at a slower pace or who are struggling are put in another class. The practice is considered controversial as it is a form of segregation.

In the United States and Canada, tracking is mainly used in high schools. Students can take more advanced classes in subjects of their choosing or in subjects that will help them get into college and university. When done well, tracking allows teachers to tailor lessons to meet the needs of the class. It gives everyone a chance to learn at a comfortable pace.

Students who learn more quickly often get great results when placed in the same class. This is because they are given more challenging assignments. On the other hand, students who do not do as well in school face greater risks. The course work is less challenging and of a poorer quality. The teachers may not have the skills to address the needs of students who require more support.

BEYOND THE SCHOOL WALLS

In Canada, studies show that students from high-income families enter the school system much better prepared than children from low-income families. Children from higher income homes have better access to early childhood programs with qualified caregivers who help them to learn to read and write. Also, Canadian provinces differ in their support of preschool education.

WHAT'S AT STAKE?

Some parents believe they can provide a better education for their children through homeschooling. What are the benefits of homeschooling? Are there any concerns?

▼ Locker Project, founded by Katie Wallace, helps provide about 1,000 children in Maine with nutritious meals to help improve their learning capacity, health, and future. Not every school or community can do this.

Whether students have help at home and in their community also plays a part in education equality. For instance, are their parents able to help them with their homework? Do the students speak the language of teaching at home? Do they face discrimination or have physical or mental disabilities that require special assistance? Are they eating a balanced meal at the start of their day?

▶ The U.S. No Child Left Behind Act of 2001 tried to give equal opportunities to disadvantaged children in public schools. It raised graduation rates but was controversial because it penalized schools that struggled to raise standards or were too focused on tests.

COST OF GOING TO COLLEGE IN U.S.A.–PER YEAR
Based on figures for full tuition and fees for 2018–2019

The vast difference in cost of college education adds to education inequality.

$35,676

$21,629

$9,716

| Public, In-State 2-year course | Public, Out-of-State 2-year course | Private 4-year course |

Worldwide, more than 260 million primary-age children get no schooling. About 54 percent of these children live in **sub-Saharan Africa**. Another 274 million primary-age children are not learning the basic skills they need to lead healthy and productive lives.

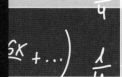

▼ In May 2019, protestors in New York challenged U.S. Secretary of Education Betsy DeVos, who pushed for the privatization of public schools and proposed big cuts to federal education funding, among other related changes.

FOCUSED RESEARCH

Statistics surrounding education equality, such as these, are constantly shifting and changing, as are facts and opinions on the topic. With every new survey, study, or event that takes place, there is something new to learn. Therefore, it is important not only to get informed, but also to stay informed.

As an informed citizen, you can make better decisions in your day-to-day life. Some good source materials for learning about education equality and what impacts it include:

- Reading brochures from nonprofit groups that work with schools to improve equal education at local and international levels. Among these are *JumpStart* and *Learning Forward* in the United States, and *Indspire* and *An Aid to Help Foundation* in Canada.
  - Listening to podcasts, such as *The Bell* and *The Through Line,* that share perspectives on the school system from students and educators.
  - Following education experts like Andreas Schleicher, Bill Ayers, and Maria Luz Torre.
- Visiting the websites of equal education advocacy units such as *Education Post, EdVoice,* and the *Center on Reinventing Public Education.*
- Reading reports on education from global organizations, for example UNICEF, the World Bank, the Organisation for Economic Co-operation and Development (OECD), UNESCO, and Education International.
- Watching documentary films such as *Waiting for "Superman"* (see page 11).

THE CENTRAL ISSUES

The U.S. National Bureau of Economic Research found that an increase of about 20 percent per student in school funding can lead to 25 percent higher earnings as an adult and a 20 percent decrease in adult poverty. So why might the government choose not to spend more on education?

International organizations, such as the World Bank, OECD, and UNESCO, conduct research projects on global education. They develop standards, policies, and regulations for the education sector in the hope of bringing about positive changes.

Nonprofit groups also work to improve the education situation in countries around the world. One of these, Education International, is made up of more than 32 million education professionals from 179 countries and territories. The organization promotes free, quality public education for everyone and fights against racism and discrimination in schools. Another nonprofit, Global Partnership for Education (GPE), partners with donor governments, other organizations, and teachers in more than 60 countries. Since GPE was founded in 2002, it has helped put about 22 million children in school and increased global literacy rates to 81 percent.

NORTH AMERICAN INITIATIVES

There are both government-sponsored and community-based initiatives across North America that focus on education equality. In the United States, the federally funded Every Student Succeeds Act came into effect in 2015 to help ensure disadvantaged children have every opportunity to succeed in school. The goal of the program was to ensure all children receive a high-quality education.

In the mid-1990s, the government of Canada started the Aboriginal Head Start in Urban and Northern Communities (AHSUNC) Program to support the learning and development needs of children living in First Nations, Inuit, and Métis communities. The program receives about $50 million a year to help with education, health, culture and language, nutrition, social support, and parental involvement programs.

THE CENTRAL ISSUES

When people are misinformed about the facts, they may come to unfair conclusions or become complacent. They may believe there is nothing they can do to change the situation in their own communities or in other parts of the world. How can you become more informed about education equality in your community?

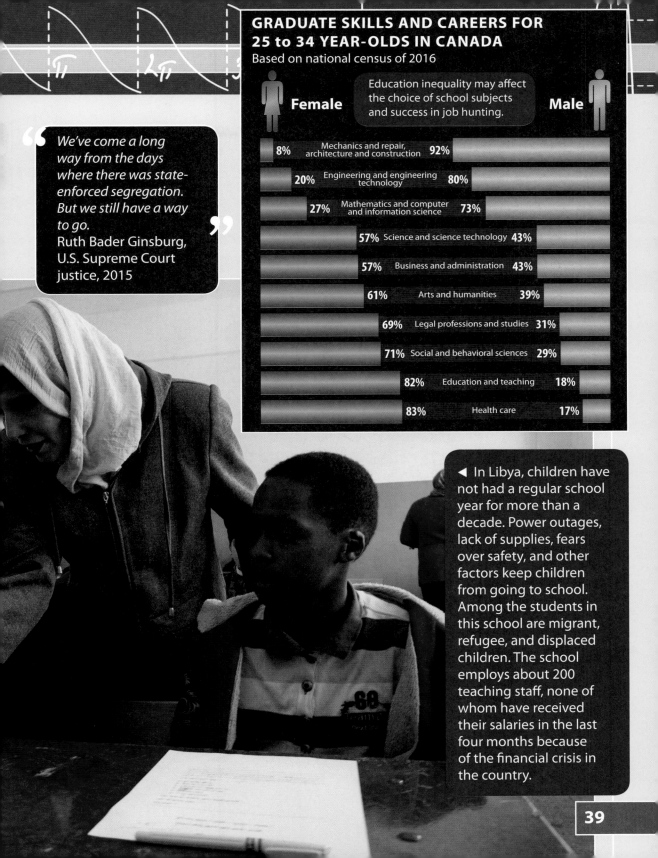

GRADUATE SKILLS AND CAREERS FOR 25 to 34 YEAR-OLDS IN CANADA
Based on national census of 2016

Female

Male

Education inequality may affect the choice of school subjects and success in job hunting.

Female	Subject	Male
8%	Mechanics and repair, architecture and construction	92%
20%	Engineering and engineering technology	80%
27%	Mathematics and computer and information science	73%
57%	Science and science technology	43%
57%	Business and administration	43%
61%	Arts and humanities	39%
69%	Legal professions and studies	31%
71%	Social and behavioral sciences	29%
82%	Education and teaching	18%
83%	Health care	17%

We've come a long way from the days where there was state-enforced segregation. But we still have a way to go.
Ruth Bader Ginsburg, U.S. Supreme Court justice, 2015

◄ In Libya, children have not had a regular school year for more than a decade. Power outages, lack of supplies, fears over safety, and other factors keep children from going to school. Among the students in this school are migrant, refugee, and displaced children. The school employs about 200 teaching staff, none of whom have received their salaries in the last four months because of the financial crisis in the country.

6 PLAN OF ACTION

It is important to think critically about topics such as education equality, and to act upon your investigation. Creating a **news diet** will help you considerably. Use a selection of media, including the Internet, to provide you with a constant influx of information from across the globe. Use that data to evolve a plan of action.

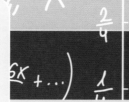

INTERNET SEARCHES

When looking at websites, address extensions can help identify the sources of the information:

.gov (government)—official government organizations or departments. You may not be able to access all areas of these websites.

.org (organization)—usually nonprofit organizations and charities. You may have to register to use these.

.com (commercial)—mostly businesses. It is the most widely used web address extension.

Country extensions:

.ca Canada
.us United States
.au Australia
.uk United Kingdom
.ru Russia
.de Germany

◄ A study conducted by Eleanor Armour-Thomas in New York City showed that schools with large marginalized or underprivileged populations scored as well as students from more advantaged communities when they had highly skilled teachers.

CREATING YOUR OWN NEWSFEED

While it is important to check local news programs and newspapers to learn about the state of education in your own community, it is also good to look for sources of information that tell you what education is like in other parts of the country or the world. This will broaden your view of the issue and see how different sets of factors and circumstances can make people come to a range of conclusions. Your view may support or oppose the common opinion, but if you are well informed, your view matters just as much.

Use this list of source materials to help you stay informed about education equality issues:

- Tune into fact-based TV programs on CNN, PBS NewsHour, CTV National News, and The National
- Read articles in credible newspapers and magazines such as *The New York Times*, the *National Post*, *Time*, *Maclean's*, and *The Guardian*.
- Talk with friends, family, and educators about current affairs. Be open to new perspectives.
- Set up a Google alert for news stories about education equality and education policies so you always have the latest information.
- Tune into radio interviews, panels, and discussions with international organizations, world leaders, and governments.
- Listen to podcasts by students and educators about their own experiences in the school system.
- Volunteer to work with groups that help underserved and disadvantaged youth.
- Meet with people who do not share your own point of view on the topic to discuss their views.

Based on the fundamental rights presented in the UDHR (see page 15), everyone deserves the right to equal education. Access to equitable education helps break the cycle of poverty, leads to better health and well-being, encourages everyone to be part of society, and raises the standard of living.

In an equal education system, everyone has the same opportunities. It is what they make of them that matters. Students who put in less effort or those who are naturally good at learning will have different success rates. Many countries in Europe and Asia provide funding to schools through a central government. This often allows for more consistent and fair opportunities since schools receive funding based on the number of students no matter their social status. However, this can also lead to unequal opportunities in such places where there are many immigrant children not fluent in the language used in their schooling.

Supporters of educational equality hold that education is not equal if the government only meets the minimum human rights guidelines that indicate "every child has a right to go to school." They believe education equality means giving children what they need to achieve, which leads to some children getting more because they need more. This is equity.

HOW CAN YOU HELP

Building awareness of education equality issues and how they impact you, your family and friends, and the people in your community will help you appreciate the many perspectives involved. It will also allow you to make better choices and decisions about other important issues. Together, they will help you become a better citizen.

▶ On February 19, 2019, students in Toronto, Canada, rallied against cuts to the Ontario Student Assistance Program, which provides loans and grants to help students pay for their college or university education.

WHAT'S AT STAKE?

All countries around the world struggle with the concept of education equality. Often, girls, refugees, LGBTQ youth, and disabled people do not experience equal education opportunities. What would the concept look like if governments and other organizations were to ensure the rights of marginalized groups?

SEARCH TIPS

In search windows on the Internet:

• Use quotation marks around a phrase to find that exact combination of words (for example, "education equality").

• Use the minus sign to eliminate certain words from your search (for example, Education -private).

• Use a colon and an extension to search a specific site (for example, Education:.gov for all government website mentions of the topic).

• Use the word Define and a colon to search for word definitions (for example, Define: equity).

GLOSSARY

alternative A different way of doing things

assimilate Become more like others; to fit into a group

atrocities Actions that are extremely cruel

bias Favoring one perspective over another

binding law An agreement between people with legal requirements they must meet

compensation Reward for service or payment for damage

constitution Written laws and rules by which a country is governed

context The setting in which an event happens

controversy Argument over a certain matter

current affairs Events happening now

curriculum Lessons and activities taught in schools

discrimination Acting badly against a specific group

doctrine Principle, belief, or policy held by a government, or other group

Emancipation Proclamation Order issued by President Lincoln in 1863 that freed enslaved people

enslaved Person owned by another and treated as property, without any rights

equal Having the same status, rights, and opportunities as everyone else

equitably Treated in a way that is fair

evaluating Judging or determining the value of something

fundamental The main foundation on which something is based

harassment Unwanted verbal or physical behavior that is meant to hurt or offend someone

home economics Lessons that teach skills that are useful for managing a home

immigrants People who enter a country from other countries to live there permanently

independent Free from control by another country

indigenous The original inhabitants, or First Peoples

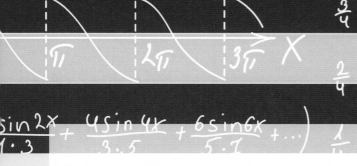

information literacy Skill in using good source material to reach balanced conclusions

LGBTQ Acronym for lesbian, gay, bisexual, transgender, and queer or questioning

mandate Command or order from a government

marginalized Ignored or left out

news diet The group of sources you use to get your news

perspectives Point of view or attitude toward something

post-secondary Term for college and university education

potential Having or showing the capacity to develop into something in the future

prospectuses Printed booklets advertising schools or universities to potential parents or students

residential schools Government-funded religious schools for indigenous children in Canada

segregation Separating races through inferior treatment

society People living and working together in a country in an organized way

source material Original documents or other pieces of evidence that are studied and analyzed to get informed

statistics The collection, analysis, and presentation of numerical data often in the form of charts, tables, and graphics

sub-Saharan Africa The part of Africa that is south of the Sahara and where most of the global poor live

summary A brief statement of the main points

underprivileged People who do not have the same rights, advantages, and opportunities as others in society

United Nations An intergovernmental organization formed in 1945 and made up of more than 190 Member States and territories; it aims to maintain world peace and security

welfare Financial support provided by the government to people in need

SOURCE NOTES

QUOTATIONS

p. 4: https://www.achievement.org/achiever/sonia-sotomayor/

p. 7: Cited in Howe, William A. and Penelope L. Lisi. *Becoming a Multicultural Educator: Developing Awareness, Gaining Skills, and Taking Action.* Sage Publications, 2016.

p. 12: https://www.newtimes.co.rw/section/read/96185

p. 21: https://tinyurl.com/y3fs8wla

p. 29: https://moaaa.dc.gov/page/malcolm-x

p. 31: Franklin, Benjamin. *Poor Richard's Almanac*, 1758.

p. 39: https://onedaywithwomen.com/female-role-model-ruth-bader-ginsburg/

REFERENCES USED FOR THIS BOOK

Chapter 1 Global Issues, pages 4–7

https://tinyurl.com/yxdvsoen
https://tinyurl.com/y422eean
https://tinyurl.com/pnz9prs
https://tinyurl.com/y4k4ch84

Chapter 2: How to Get Informed, pages 8–13

https://tinyurl.com/y9879em6
https://tinyurl.com/y5h9a8kw
https://tinyurl.com/yyozsfye
https://tinyurl.com/y6ff225o

Chapter 3: The Big Picture, pages 14–25

https://tinyurl.com/y3ekxvje
https://tinyurl.com/y6ygo5uj
https://tinyurl.com/y45xqmeu
https://tinyurl.com/y3x87h2w
https://tinyurl.com/ybstd6cs
https://tinyurl.com/y56js3nh
https://tinyurl.com/yxtqo7a5
https://tinyurl.com/y6rm4lvm
https://tinyurl.com/yxonoc5d
https://tinyurl.com/y3p4vzos
https://tinyurl.com/yxebzdnm

Chapter 4: An Informed Decision, pages 26–35

https://tinyurl.com/y6facvvs
https://tinyurl.com/y96umlr8
https://tinyurl.com/y3b5ut8f
https://tinyurl.com/y22cm6hk
https://tinyurl.com/y3jzmljv
https://tinyurl.com/y5xpkjlb
https://tinyurl.com/y65ebh2e
https://tinyurl.com/yyyxkumr

Chapter 5: Staying Informed, pages 36–39

https://tinyurl.com/y65qdwd6
https://tinyurl.com/y2bxeskq
https://tinyurl.com/yxv9jadj
https://tinyurl.com/yxgzcyrr
https://tinyurl.com/y6jl68y8
https://tinyurl.com/yd26l9l7

Chapter 6: Plan of Action, pages 40–43

https://tinyurl.com/y22nbkud

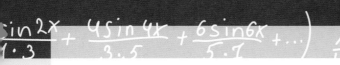

FIND OUT MORE

Finding good source material on the Internet can sometimes be a challenge. When analyzing how reliable the information is, consider these points:

- Who is the author of the page? Is it an expert in the field or a person who experienced the event?
- Is the site well known and up to date? A page that has not been updated for several years probably has out-of-date information.
- Can you verify the facts with another site? Always double-check information.

- Have you checked all possible sites? Don't just look on the first page a search engine provides.
- Remember to try government sites and research papers.
- Have you recorded website addresses and names? Keep this data so you can backtrack later and verify the information you want to use.

WEBSITES

Find out more about the role gender plays in education equality:
https://en.unesco.org/themes/education-and-gender-equality

Learn what parents, educators, and others are doing to prevent funding cuts to education in Ontario, Canada:
https://www.buildingbetterschools.ca/

Discover what the U.S. Department of Education is doing to achieve equity:
https://www.ed.gov/equity

Explore what it means to be tolerant and understanding of everyone's education rights:
https://www.tolerance.org/

Meet teachers who advocate for the equal treatment of all students:
https://edtrust.org/

BOOKS

Anderson, Carol and Tonya Bolden. *We Are Not Yet Equal: Understanding Our Racial Divide.* Bloomsbury YA, 2018.

Boyce, Jo Ann Allen and Debbie Levy. *This Promise of Change: One Girl's Story in the Fight for School Equality.* Bloomsbury Children's Books, 2019.

Bridges, Ruby. *Through My Eyes.* Scholastic Press, 1999.

Levine, Kristine. *The Lions of Little Rock.* Putnam's Sons Books for Young Readers, 2012.

Yousafzai, Malala, and Patricia McCormick. *I Am Malala: How One Girl Stood Up for Education and Changed the World.* Thorndike Press, 2017.

ABOUT THE AUTHOR

Heather C. Hudak has written hundreds of books for children. When she is not writing, she enjoys traveling the world and spending time with her husband and their many rescue cats and dogs.

INDEX